Music Madness
for Middle School

Lynn Howard

authorHOUSE®

AuthorHouse™
1663 Liberty Drive
Bloomington, IN 47403
www.authorhouse.com
Phone: 1-800-839-8640

First published by AuthorHouse 11/7/2011

ISBN: 978-1-4670-6716-4 (e)
ISBN: 978-1-4670-6715-7 (sc)

Library of Congress Control Number: 2011919107

Printed in the United States of America

Any people depicted in stock imagery provided by Thinkstock are models, and such images are being used for illustrative purposes only. Certain stock imagery © Thinkstock.

Help Us Save The Program!

My thanks to the editors: Colette Lease and Lorie McCarter.
My special thanks to my partner and wife, Carol.

A heap of gratitude to the many music teachers
who fought or are fighting the good fight.

Lynn Howard

Table of Contents

Music in Our Western World-
A Classroom Philosophy

Background

Yes, music did touch my early years. Mother played the piano and stud-ied voice. I took clarinet in elementary school and sang a little in junior high. I did take piano lessons from fourth grade until my dad tired of forcing me to practice. As the hormones flooded my overweight frame, I determined to "be a man". Therefore, I left music behind and it disap-peared from my life during my sophomore year in high school. When I was a senior at Central Washington University (1959) , I had to take a general music "appreciation" course, fortunately, for only a quarter. As graduation approached, I looked for a coaching job with a high school teaching position. I finally realized that I had to enter into a district through an elementary teaching job. Now I found myself in strange situations: playing piano for a choir in both elementary school and at my next job, junior high. After three years of teaching history at the junior high level, I went to the University of Washington on a sabbatical leave and studied Russian language, history, and literature. When I returned to teaching I moved to a high school as language and history teacher and as an assistant football coach.

As I began my first year in the new position, there was an odd turn of events. The high school was suddenly without a choral teacher. The principal knew that I had played the piano a bit at lower levels, so he asked me to "baby sit" the class! I loved it! This was 1967 and I was thirty years old. I was teaching music and choral classes but without any training. I was hungry to find answers so I returned to Central Washington with a driving passion to learn. I took nothing for granted, truly a marvelous puzzle. I loved theory classes: much to the disbelief of the undergrads around me! At the same time, my focus began to grow toward the idea of "involvement" in music for students. I felt involvement had to happen before experience, even before knowledge, could come into play. So I started my thirty years of study, teaching, principalship and building music programs here and in New Zealand. My journey in music crossed all grades in two districts. It included choral programs to band programs in several schools I have taught music from Twinkle, Twinkle Little Star to the Bach Magnificat in D Major (rehearsing with area symphony members, to accompany the students). Working small groups with jazz and even Persichetti! I had an M.A. in Voice Performance and a love for great music.

As fate would have it, the last job for me was a middle school music situation. This job logically followed from my experience in New Zealand where I had been a part of a national "think tank" in music for the classroom tackling how to deal with 12-14 year old students in a class labeled "Music". The image of music has not always been appealing to the male gender: whether in the Northern or Southern hemisphere. Fortunately, I had either played or coached various sports my entire teaching career. This has helped to validate music for many young men.

The Problem

Besides the image of music, we now face a challenging problem in our country: resolving the place of fine arts in the curriculum. The importance of music is constantly challenged in light of the strong academic tests now taking place in our state schools. In many districts, music is literally hanging on by a thread or has been cut from the curriculum.

This problem, in my opinion evolves from "shaky academic justification", which in the eyes of some pressure groups is that classroom music is only good when it's used as a 'babysitting function', particularly with middle school students. It is often paired with P.E. classes in scheduling and therefore is usually either a trimester or a semester long. Consequently, we rarely get to work with a group of students longer than a semester. The students we have will, most likely, not be involved with any more directed or formal music in their school career. We, then, have the privilege and responsibility to present the world of music in a form they will remember and enjoy! At the age of 12-14, the education of these students presents a formidable problem.

Considering the limited time frame and most likely a "captive" and, perhaps, unwilling audience; it is necessary to decide on priorities concerning a vast field of knowledge. I also felt the necessity to offer the middle school student an incentive for diligent work. The decision was to take the last period or session (if on block schedule) for the week and make it the students' "Listening Day": a chance to listen, respect, and enjoy each other's music. Let me say that this portion of the program was possible since I held class in a portable far away from classrooms and I had a supportive principal.

The Last To Be Treated First

Listening Day-It was a "free time" for them to sit around the room and talk quietly or play games or read or do school work while they listened. I did not work on the focus factor of music at this time: I let them have that freedom. In retrospect I find it surprising that no one danced or even tried! This was a chance for a student to share their "inner self".

3

One's choice of music shows one's own thoughts and feelings: this was a safe place. By the way, I sat with them and talked to individuals, especially students who rarely communicated.

A "disc jockey" was chosen for the day. The students were allowed to bring their own CDs (tapes,also) and play selections: as long as the words were acceptable (that's 'teacher talk'-they would say, 'no cussin'). It was a very interesting problem for our students: I remember one eighth grade boy looking at a CD case with over a dozen CDs and commenting sadly that he couldn't play one of them! The students did well, though, finding a "radio" version or an artist who performed acceptable words or chose only the acceptable cuts on their CD{i.e.: Bone, Thugs, and Harmony, original album: "Crossroads"). They constantly tested my consistency. A student would, either knowingly or unknowingly give the "DJ" a CD with a "word". I would look up from my talking time with someone and EVERY eye in the room would be on me-looking for my reaction-as I told the DJ to turn it off! It was amazing how many students listened but did not "HEAR". We will deal with this later on. Through this listening time, we gained respect for each other's music. Many types of music were brought, some not played until some words of appreciation were given. The term "acceptable" came to apply to the subject of the words as well as individual words. It worked.

The predominance of music our students listened to the last five to six years was hip-hop and related (what I call) soft rap. Alternative or classic rock was brought by only a small minority. Very few brought street rap or hard rap. One had to be quite courageous to bring anything "different". One boy once brought a country CD hidden in his school bag. He had me keep it for him, but it was never played. The few "rockers" would bring alternative or acid rock but would have to assert themselves to have equal playing time. It was an interesting commentary on our musical culture today. I learned a great deal about our students and I never felt it wasted time.

When I talked to former students in the high school next door, one of the things they often mention is the Listening Day when we shared music during that last part of the week. (I substituted often in that particular high school next to the middle school where I taught.) The music choices of the students you deal with will probably be very different but, when you, as the teacher listen and appreciate, it becomes easier for the student to return the favor during the weekly class times. One last word as we start on this adventure: this program was used for all sixth, seventh, and eighth grade students in the school unless they were band students.

Objective

As middle school and junior high programs are flooded with academic pressure and many of the creative or hands-on courses disappear from the curriculum, I feel the administrators are welcoming music (along with P.E.) courses as a break for the student from the academic pressure. Mind you, it is quite easy to interject academic skills into the music curriculum. On a limited basis, this can help justifying the course. However, my goal is to offer a music course which involves creativity, hands-on work, and some academic concepts without stressing formal music structure and notation. I've divided the course into five major areas:

I. Listening and Hearing   IV. Music In Our Life

II. Creating/Performance   V. Samples of Music Activities

III. Brief History of Music

Classroom/Listening-
You Can Hear But Can You Listen?!

Ray Palmer, Band Director, Music Teacher, and my former teaching partner in New Zealand says it well:

"Have you been to a party lately and watched the conversation taking place? Everyone is talking, but no one seems to be listening! It is a sign of our times I guess. Listening is now a skill that has to be taught."

"So how do you do it? What is the magic skill called listening and how do you teach it?" Hence comes the theme for these sessions: I hear but don't listen.

Ray goes on, "TV and technical listening devices make our young generation hear sound as background but not actually listen to it. For example, while I am writing this, I cannot have music playing in the background because I listen to it-the shape of the phrase, the chord changes, the rhythm, the texture; etc-I hear AND listen!"

W. Michael Jaap, Jazz pianist extraordinaire and music teacher states, "Music is communication. It is true in ALL music, and especially true in jazz. Always try to listen closely for this communication! Then decide for yourself what the music is saying to you. Finally then, and simply, react to it!"

YOU CAN HEAR, BUT CAN YOU LISTEN?

Whatever we do in life, we spend almost 2/3 of our waking hours using our ears. So you watch the weather report and miss tomorrow's forecast! You hear the teacher talk but miss tomorrow's assignment. Focusing in the listening process of 12 to 14 year-olds can be almost non-existent.

The Classroom Process/Teaching the Concepts of Learning

A. Try some of these for openers:

Ask: What happens when we close our eyes?

What happens when we open them?

Can we shut our ears to what we hear?

Do our ears "focus" the same way as our eyes do?

Could you say, "seeing with your ears'?

What do we do fastest? Talk, think, read, or write or hear?

We hear quickly and "translate" what we hear: we're selective so to speak. We tend to memorize that chosen portion more quickly.

B. The world in which we live is full of sounds and many people don't notice them.

Experiment:

1. Have the students keep quite still and shut their eyes for about a minute (or more). Have them listen carefully.

2. Afterwards have them take a pencil and make two lists:
   a. Sounds you can recognize
   b. Sounds you can describe but do not recognize or understand.
3. Project the examples of the list for the class. Discuss, particularly, the second list.
4. Take this experiment outside have them work in groups. Have them bring back the list into the class and discuss the results.

Have the students keep a music notebook/portfolio. Have them copy the following "Hints for Listening":

1. "Focus (point) your ears" at a particular sound.
2. Keep the sounds in front of you.
3. Eliminate distractions and close your eyes.

C. After presenting this, give the students a sound/audio test. With a recorder, find ten sound such as a jet taking off, the wind, someone hammering; etc. Ask the students to write their impression of what they hear. Give the answers and discuss the sounds afterwards.

D. Tell the story of composer, John Cage. He went into an an-echoic chamber. A padded room with totally sealed walls and door. He tried to find the quietest place man could make for himself. When the room was sealed, he heard two distinct sounds, one high and one low. The sounds were continuous—he was puzzled. When he left the room he asked what were the sounds. The tech said that the high one was his nervous system and the low one was his blood in circulation! (Sound, Soundscape, p. 5)

Challenge the class to see how they could hear if they were perfectly quiet. Have them be quiet, close their eyes, and after one minute, list any sounds they heard. The discussion afterwards can be very interesting. Don't let them get silly. Keep it serious.

What sounds are we likely to hear?......not to hear?

Why do blind people seem to hear more and better?

E. Some people use sound in very different ways.

1. Here is one very different example: Yoko Ono was the wife of one of the Beatles, John Lennon. She asked a very strange requirement when "listening" to her music. She said the only sound that existed for her is in the mind. Her music only started "music' in the mind: " **Collecting Piece** – Collect sounds in your mind that you have overheard through the week. Repeat the sounds in your mind, in different orders, one afternoon. 1963" (Sound, Soundscape, p.9)

2. "A 'silent' noise weapon has been invented that can kill humans up to five miles away. The director of Britain's Noise Abatement Society said the weapon was a giant whistle powered by compressed air which projects sounds too low to be heard by the human ear but critically related to brain rhythms." (Sound, p.11)

3. Find some action pictures, have the students express the sounds in the picture. Allow them to do it in their own way-this might take a private hearing (away from the class). I had them work in pairs and choose which picture they would do. When they came to the front, I had them stand next to the piano –along with the noise of others trying and planning-this allowed them to make their sounds in "private". I wish I had had a candid camera for that one! (The faces they make are quite entertaining!) They can try to hear a sound in their mind.

4. Try this routine with some sounds: record a place in a video or a movie where there is no talking. Practice: Listening, Perceiving, Remembering, Responding, Evaluating! When a person focuses ones ears, one will be surprised how many different sounds are heard. One will select, analyze, and order automatically when listening. This is the process of perceiving or making sense of a sound or a series of sounds. Normally, most only remember about half of what they hear.

5. We need to:
   a. Listen several times
   b. Write words, descriptions, make doodle reactions and reminders
   c. Tap the rhythm
   d. We need to sing it or repeat it.
   e. Review again, compare with the recording

This will help!

F. Constantly keep the "Hints for Listening" in front of the students: posted somewhere in the room if possible.

Play contemporary examples which have emotional content-no words-let them discuss" what is the music 'saying'?" Ask the students to bring examples on tapes or CDs. Constantly point out: music does communicate. You could discuss the effect of rock, disco beat, rap beat on the heart; etc.

The students need to understand that there are more ways to communicate than by simply using words.

Creating-
Our Own Music!

There are many ways to express oneself in music. The student can bring music into being as easily as any composer. One of the methods used in other countries more than the United States is " graphic composition". Composition formed on as a graph (Appendixes 2,3,4,5). The graph has original performance symbols created by the student (s) composer (s) or professional composers. You need to answer some questions about your class in order to get an indication of how much you'll be able to challenge them in this curriculum. Use these questions along with the student project:

As an introduction have some students try the work in Appendix 1a, using the piano.

1. Can they follow the directions? Can they "perform" it?
2. Can they observe the difference when different people do it.
3. Do they understand the symbols made by the students or others? Can different ones be used?
4. Could other instruments be used? (Appendix 1b)

Introduce available percussion instruments and discuss their sound potential. Let individuals have a go-always stress control. Also stress care of instruments. A stop watch or a digital wrist watch to time the compositions would be necessary.

Oh, a note about the piano, I was able to take the front off the old studio piano we had and let the students use the strings without key or pedal control. They can use their fists too. If they are gentle, they can run up and down the keys ; etc.. There's many ways to approach the instrument situation The students could learn to make their own instruments or bring inexpensive or play instruments from home (all named and in a container).

A relatively good recorder is a key component since all "compositions" need to be recorded and replayed and discussed (not criticized). I find you could even use one of the hand-held digital recorders from Radio Shack. Set the volume carefully: it will pick up every sound. Some are hard to operate, you'll need to be ready to use it.

Once you feel secure in having enough different instruments (some-where between 10 and 15) the next step is to allow the students to form into groups of four or five each. Work with those who don't care for group-work. It is best to get them placed with one group or another: doing something!

A. Once the groups are established, it is time to begin sharing the struc-ture of the "project". You needn't say it often, but the formal name of the groups is Graphic Composition Groups.

B. The students will need help assigning tasks so it's probably necessary to have a chart or write the list on the board.

1. They need to choose a leader: a conductor.
2. The group chooses artists to layout and color the graph follow-ing the desire of the group (refer to D2) - each instrument has

its own line and own symbols on the graph (refer to Appendix 2a and 2b).

3. All except the conductor will probably need to be an "instrumentalist".

4. If one in the group doesn't feel to be an "instrumentalist", they could work the recording process.

C. Before any "performance", the role of the listener or observer needs to be discussed.

1. The necessity for strict quietness needs to be stressed: "This is your recording studio."

2. It is just good non-judgmental manners to always show appreciation with applause at the end of the performance.

3. No negativity is expressed unless guided through analysis by the teacher.

D. The Composition

1. For the first composition, give an easy assignment: one emotion (happiness, sadness; etc.) The assignment is to be 30 seconds long. They can leave it one section or divide it into 3 sections of 10 seconds each or 2 sections of 15 seconds. Their choice. The sections are short so it will be a challenge.

2. The students will need a sheet (perhaps two) of 11 by 22 construction paper-of a lighter color. They will need crayons or colored ink pens or markers. Have newspaper spread in areas where they could do their composition artwork. Students are to create their own symbols for the instruments. Only the students in the group need to understand them and each student will have his own instrumental line to follow.

3. When they are done with the artwork, suggest that they might practice. Have them take turns with a limited number of instruments.

4. The conductor has to have a watch with a digital face. (I used to lend my watch to each group) You may, at this time, train the conductor to move the players to the next section of the chart as the time expires in the section being "played".

Let me break away from procedures for a moment and say that it should be obvious by now that if the instructor/teacher has had formal music training, that now has to be put aside! And like John Cage, American modernistic composer, you have to be open to a totally new approach and treat it seriously. They will quickly read your attitude through speech, facial expression, and body language. I always got very "irritated" when there was even a whisper before or during the recording-it was always:"STOP, WHAT'S THAT NOISE!?! NOW WE HAVE TO DO IT AGAIN!!!" If they insist on rudeness, stop and take the privilege of recording/creating music and listening on Friday (temporarily) and go on to other portions of the program (to be dealt with later).

E. Performance (after perhaps 15 minutes of rehearsal or quicker if things are getting out of hand)

1. Get the first group arranged closely to the recording device. (refer to Appendix 4)

2. The conductor needs a music stand—he/she will have to turn it facing the group and place the composition on the stand. The composition needs to be seen by all in the group so the colors have to be dark and big enough.

3. While standing behind the music stand facing the group, the conductor (with his/her timing device) has to start the group then point over the stand to each section of the work moving the

pointer as the digital timer dictates. And then he/she has to cut them off at the end. It will move quickly with only 30 seconds planned! (Appendix 4)

Note: I find that the best "pointer" is just for the conductor to use their finger.

F. Post-performance

1. Play the recording afterwards-don't discuss reaching the goal the first time, just let them hear themselves. I usually graded them on: did they or didn't they do it.
2. As they go on to more sophisticated creations, you can put them on the spot, so to speak:
   a. Did you (the group) practice?
   b. Could you "read " the music?
   c. Did the composition do what it was supposed to do? (Address their frustrations, such as the shortness of the piece; etc.)
   d. Do address the audience and compliment them on their quietness; etc. Ask for positive comments.
3. My suggestion is to give them another single emotion but give them a longer time frame such as a minute. Let them break the sections into whatever they think they might need.
4. If the project isn't good or not successful, do another example, next time using a different emotion or idea.

G. The Next Step Up is to try two emotions for contrast (Appendix 5).

1. You probably need to go to a longer piece and have them widen the changes-use your imagination and theirs! Do as many as possible interspersed with the rest of the curriculum.

2.   The perfect culminating project would be to add a line of words-as shown in the Appendix. I used the poetry book of Tupoc Shukur (would you believe) for examples of words. His suspicious connections and rap music did not deter him from being a surprisingly good "word smith". The poetry book is quite interesting.

3.   Point to Appendix 2a and 2b for a good example of the use of words. You might furnish some books from the library or other sources to help. These compositions are particularly good to share

I remember two interesting examples of eighth grade creativity. One boy brought his laptop computer to the class and used a music program he had as one of the instruments in the composition for his group! I remember, when the program was just getting started, an African-American girl tall, very stately, and very popular. She took six of the boys in the class who had fought being too involved –organized them, handed them instruments, shared her poetry, and rehearsed them! They were able to align the words and the "music". The performance was quite good! All of a sudden they were motivated.

My first short "retirement" came when I finished at this middle school. During the next year, I substituted at the high school next door. As I had many of the students in class whom I knew from middle school, I noticed that there were often positive comments about the music class-they remembered special parts and special times. Since I had only seen most of them for only a trimester, it was interesting to me to see so many students with good memories associated with music.

History Of Music-
Was It Really Like That?!

After the first year of the music curriculum, we were asked to incorporate into our program some amount of language arts practices. I considered several things but arrived at the idea of talking about composers and musicians with the students. My routine was to put a somewhat formal outline on the white board (computer or smart board). If the students copied the outline while I talked, they could receive an A grade! As I talked, they were given other examples to write in if they so wished. This was cultural shock because they were not used to writing in the general music class (many were not used to receiving A's either). I also gave another A if the students not only took down notes but also filled in the outline. My last method of "inspiration" was to place the history period the session before the students listening session with the promise to take away the listening or part of the listening if history wasn't done well.

Since one or two would occasionally rebel against writing, I would usually do the history portion of the course on the day before Listening Period. This added weight to the session as they had to produce in order to have their "free time" on the next day.

Baroque Period

I also found the outline helpful to keep me on task as I told the story of Bach's life in narrative form. I usually highlighted important or interesting points: i.e.: the immense size of Bach's family. Yes, the Baroque Period was first. Since the Baroque Period is so different in many ways from other classical periods, I usually began with an overall look at styles, art, instruments, and anything else which illustrated the ornamental aspect of the time. There are some spectacular books with excellent pictures and examples available. The music does appeal to the students also as the bass line comes to the fore. (A model of Baroque presentation is in the Appendix 8a and 8b).

My routine (you may certainly adopt your own) was to put a formal outline on the board: relevant Baroque aspects and then follow in the next outline session with the life of Bach and his Music. I stayed fairly brief on the original profile outline.

As I talked about the aspects or the composer, I would fill in the outline in a brief way. I would also play examples of the music. I think it is important not to play too much of the example but to show or illustrate the point you are trying to make. There is a vast library of Bach's music and also of the other Baroque composer I shared: Handel. Some students may be able to relate to such as the Hallelujah Chorus. I had a tendency to focus on the magnificent church organs and the music of the era. Pictures of the architecture and common things such as a clock or a window-the elaborateness of it all was interesting to the students.

Classical Period

Beethoven is often listed in the Classical section (as well as Romantic, in his later compositions). (Appendix 9b) I "moved" him to the Romantic era and focused strongly on Mozart and the invention of the piano in the Classical Era. It and the use of repetition were the strong themes. It was easy to find examples of repetition in Mozart's music. I combined these aspects along with Mozart and examples into one presentation. It was interesting to talk about the harpsichord and compare it with our present piano (good to play selections of both also). Actually this could be divided into two sessions. This is certainly one of the things you could do: The compositions of his youth were always very interesting to the students. The students always seemed to like his faster pieces, as many were light and "happy sounding". I always finished with the (controversial) story of his "mysterious visitor" and Mozart's death, then I would play some of the Requiem.

Romantic Period

The students usually enjoyed the Romantic Era with emphasis on Beethoven. I encourage you to use an excellent movie available in educational music outlets called Beethoven Lives Upstairs. It is well liked. I, with the students help, made an outline of his life when the movie was over. Obviously, the boy and his mother are not real but the facts around Beethoven are very accurate. For listening, I used the beginning of Symphony #1 where he keeps "beginning" over and over again: to involve the audience and somewhat toy with listeners. I played the famous Symphony #5 theme and talked about its use during WWII to raise the morale of the country. I used this period to introduce program music and played portions of Beethoven's Sixth Symphony.

The Sixth Symphony is the story of a river from a little brooklet to a large powerful river. There are definite scenes and events (including a storm) which take place as the river flows to the sea. It would be good to get a recording that discusses these things if you are not familiar with the composition. It's important to know that all the background music in the movie is also Beethoven's.

The last piece of music I wish to mention had a very interesting introduction in the classroom, a student, during a bit of free time walked to the piano and, with one finger, played the first seven notes of Fur Elise! Before I left this particular middle school, I can't tell you how many students played that! Some knew more-one boy played the whole piece one time! They were really intrigued with this plaintive melody!

Twentieth Century

You have found one way to present modern trends in music already: the graphic composition! You could go back to Appendix 2 and Appendix 3 and show examples of contemporary music- recordings of the Penderecki, Threnody. My usual approach was to get my old VHS of John Cage and play the "Prepared Piano" selection. It's a bit of a cultural shock to students: don't let them get ideas on your piano. Some of the things Cage does with a piano does harm the strings somewhat. Maybe a little talk on the profiles of this period could be enough. I would play a little Debussy for them (or a student could possibly play something else).

The Birth of Pop Music in America, 1930-1970

As you start this section, you have to make sure the students understand the concept of "pop" in music. Too many associate the term with a particular style of music-not so! It simply means the music that people were playing or listening to-was "popular". We constantly have the challenge of keeping their minds open to many styles of music as we listen.

As we begin this section, I bring to your attention one of the most complete "histories" of pop (mostly rock) music: The Definitive Illustrated

Encyclopedia of Rock, it is an excellent compendium. It covers mostly from 1930 to the end of the century. Yes, you can probably find a more personal narrative of this or that artist but to tie it together and present an artist, yes, everybody who was involved in some sort of order is really spectacular! (Bibliography Listing)

Early Days (up to 1940s)

I picked material very much at random in this section. I started with a basic outline and then talked about Ragtime, Jazz, Big Bands, Marching Bands. I mentioned Count Basie, Benny Goodman, Dinah Washington and Duke Ellington.

I actually drew out two examples to illustrate cultural change/ferment: Scott Joplin and Louis Armstrong.

Scott Joplin's music lives today....how? The kids will tell you...."the ice cream man!!" The Maple Leaf Rag was written in 1899, in 1973, the Sting was a popular movie with ALL his music as background! Get a recording-at least of the Maple Leaf Rag- and play it. It's difficult to play-so complex- yet it sends a message..what a legacy!

Louis Armstrong sang many messages about our culture-many of the last ones were positive but I play an interesting one for the students: Mack the Knife. Here's a song that has a very charming and bright (happy?) melody line, yet the picture painted is of a grisly murder! It's sort of a "welcome to Chicago" in the 30's. You would have to do some interpreting as the words sometimes mask the actual meaning.

The Roots

As America prepared for war and became involved in war during the late 30s and most of the 40s, there was a significant immigration of blacks to the north as many job opportunities arose. So it was that music was divided racially. Literally all the radio stations were controlled by white owners. However the black population brought some new music with them: the blues. They had been in "cotton slavery", near starvation, and there was tradition to sing of the past. Several black groups began to come together and they would combine rhythm and blues. The first black group to appeal to a white audience was the Dominoes (Crying In the Chapel-1953) So R and B was the northern American movement. Cowboy singers appeared during this time: Gene Autry, Johnny Cash, Hank Williams…

The 1950's

As we start into the last half of the 20th Century, I think some things have to be said about this era: concerning both presentation and the culture. Even though I grew up during the late 40's and the early 50's, I did not realize a strict color line existed in the music/radio world. It didn't really open completely until I was in high school: 1953-5. The re-strictions of WWII lessoned as the decade wore on. The ascendency of Russia in the "space race" and the atomic revolution helped to create a "live for today-to h___ with tomorrow" attitude. Rock and roll came out of Britain, spreading over the western hemisphere. Was the established generation concerned? Look at Indonesia and Argentina-they banned the music!

Artists began to sing about parents and school-definite teen subjects (pop song: A Teenager in Love). The Sun Records in Memphis, Tennessee reigned supreme with artists such Elvis Pressley, Jerry Lee Lewis, Johnny Cash. Men's groups were prominent early on and black groups became in demand with white audiences.

I showed a good portion of the movie, Grease, during this section. An interesting thing about the movie is that one of my former music students was in the movie: Susan Buckner.

These three sections can be treated a couple ways: you do the lead outline routine, name artists and show key events or you could actually study one of the artists such as Elvis who influenced many other performers. Do an in-depth study or take the main artists and have the students take a particular one and report on it (complete with music). Let's take a look at a brief list of important artists-those who had an impact:

1. Chuck Berry-super athletic. While performing, leap to the top of the piano, jump off the stage, do a "chicken walk' all over the stage.

2. Ray Charles- combined rhythm and blues with jazz. Performed songs of social awareness (film, Ray, 2004)

3. Everly Bros.-brought country music into the scene, combining it with R and B. Influenced such artists as the Beach Boys.

4. Bill Haley, "Father of Rock and Roll". He translated black "R and B" into a form adolescent whites could understand. Two most famous songs: Shake, Rattle, and Roll and Rock Around The Clock. Popularized the term, "Rock" as a musical term. His songs were the background for two great movies: Blackboard Jungle and Happy Days.

5. Buddy Holly-first to do arranging, production as well as performing. Died tragic death early in 1959. Influenced singers such as Bob Dylan, the Beatles, Rolling Stones, and Paul Simon.

6. Elvis Pressley the best singer of black inspired R and B and country. He was the first ultimate ROCK STAR! The picture of masses of girls swooning, screaming; etc. Very influential in his crooning, country interpretations, and blues. Very controversial in his pelvic movement in performance.

25

The 1960's

This is popular music's most influential decade. The Beatles brought vast creativity from England to America and the West Coast rock boom grew with drugs. Guitars were now the instrument of choice-rock took over! Guitar genii such as Eric Clapton, Jimi Hendrix, and Duane Allman. The recording studio and its technology added to the creative process.

This is the age of "hippies" hating war /embracing "love and peace". Vast involvement in drugs came about. Dance music came from "Motown"-Detroit and Stax in Memphis. This is the decade of major festivals: the Monterey International in 1967and the first Woodstock in 1969. It was a decade that started with subdued creativity and ended with intense psychedelic colour and light shows. This is illustrated best in the performances of Jimi Hendrix, Janis Joplin, and Mick Jagger. All equaled energy and excess.

The surf craze brought us the Beach Boys. It was live big, live high, forget everything else. London brought us the Rolling Stones, the Yardbirds and many more. Prominent in Soul were Ray Charles and Aretha Franklin. Some of the most influential artists originated in Motown: Stevie Wonder and the top group, the Temptations. No doubt the Beatles influenced most people in the 60's and thereafter. But those who led the revolution in America were led by Bob Dylan, Barry McGuire, Sonny and Cher, and others. The revolution was inspired by the politics and culture of the 60's: Viet Nam, conservatism, LSD.......by the middle of the decade, rock had become an immense social creature.

(As I name various artists, I would encourage you to find some old recordings or CDs or tapes of some of the artists that you feel express the times mentioned. An example, I found an old recording of Woodstock-I played for the students Jimi Hendrix' version of the national anthem.) This becomes very important here since things really began

The Electric Revolution (Term used by music historians)

Rock begins to separate itself from pop music. When Jimi Hendrix comes to London and performs, the music with light shows and electric distortion begins to become popular. Avant garde groups like Pink Floyd, using a cash register for rhythm, become popular (I always play this one). More groups are now writing their own music and long playing albums become the norm (the three-minute record fades.) The first rock opera comes out in 1969, Tommy.

By the end of the 60's, there was great emphasis in the psychedelic realm (probably the result of drugs) and excess, disillusion, and death had replaced the celebration of "love and life". The 60's were filled with music: beginning in the 60's, the list of recording/performing artists in the Definitive Illustrated Encyclopedia of Rock begins to cover two full large pages with small writing. (footnote)

1970's –The Age of Crossovers and Crossouts (my title)

This was an age of new crazes: often short lived, artists crossing lines, louder, more psychedelic material. Glam Rock appears with groups like Alice Cooper and KISS. You have the adult social issues in music from the Eagles and Bruce Springsteen. Punk Rock and rebels plea for social change and racial harmonies. A new black icon arises and it's not rock: Bob Marley! The new, cool instrument is the synthesizer. Pink Floyd leads the progressive field with the album: Dark Side of the Moon (Money is the best cut.) Music becomes one of the all-time biggest industries in the U.S.!

1. Big outdoor concerts continued during the 70's with groups like The Band, Grateful Dead, and the Allman Bros..

2. Country became more popular: Tammy Wynette, Dolly Parton, some larger groups dabbled in country: the Byrds and especially the Eagles. Can you imagine, Hotel California (full of symbolism concerning the hopelessness of drugs) sold 28 MILLION copies!!

3. Serious and talented song writers became prominent such as Carol King, James Taylor, Carly Simon, Rod Stewart, and perhaps the most important, Elton John. They wrote introspective songs-introduced their own viewpoints.

4. The biggest rock phenom was undoubtedly Led Zeppelin (with cuts like Stairway to Heaven). Two popular groups were the Doobie Bros. and the Allman Bros.-not really family! It was tragic when Duane Allman died, ironically like Jimi Hendrix, he was one of the outstanding guitarists of the era.

5. A new black sound was becoming very popular, it was easy listening and positive in its themes. Sly and the Family Stone and Stevie Wonder were the most prominent musicians in this decade.

6. Disco became the "in" dance craze: fiery, danceable, often R and B, psychedelic effects, and radical politics. Issac Hayes, with that huge bass voice, became one of the leading lights.

7. Funk edged in through jazz origins-Earth, Wind, and Fire, some of Miles Davis.

8. Reggae was and still is very strong, even though the icon, Bob Marley, has passed on. The music, with its marking rhythms, its slow back-beat feeling, and its call for universal brotherhood is still very popular today.

9. And from those "garage bands', arose Punk Rock. It had speed, conviction, force. One author said, "filth and force", it was

vicious. It has been watered down since then and you have "new wave" vocalists such as Blondie

As you can see, in the 50s and 60s, more than several of the musicians have "crossed the line", so to speak. One of the most interesting to share with students is Eric Clapton: from Cream to Cocaine to Blues to In Heaven (when a daughter dies). Having experienced drugs, he sings about the evil of it: interesting song.You can leave Cocaine out if you want, but I find the 7th and 8th graders do "know the game", so to speak. As I write this Clapton is touring and just came through our city last week. It was $100 for a ticket to the concert. He's one of the great guitarists who's "made it through". Hopefully, he has his life on a good road now.

Probably the most interesting "pioneering" work during the 60s and into the 70s and still around today was Blood, Sweat, and Tears and the group, Chicago.

Blood, Sweat, and Tears was the first group to use brass instruments with rock compositions. They were a very talented group (the flute playing was well done also) but I guess the personalities did not come together well. So they faded but the CDs are still around, Spinning Wheel was the main cut I used for physical movement in the room-transition to another activity. The students loved it.

Chicago got their name from their original "home base". They actually lived and practiced for one year (!) in a house in Chicago before they came out public. The album Chicago IX is absolutely their best. The imaginative writing of Robert Lamm made the work a lasting effort. You can go to Borders or any music/book store and buy a copy today! Chicago does perform today but the group has gone to mostly new people-just not the same yet.

Well, this is where I usually ended this portion of the curriculum. You can certainly enlarge on various sections-ones you feel more comfortable with but the students really do well in any of the sections. You're going to have to have CDs or music recorded or however you do it. I located some music money and purchased a combination record (yes!) , tape, and CD recorder with excellent speakers. The tape- CD player was a double system and recorded both exterior and interior work. It could also record older records. It's very important to use record collectors and those who haunt the used music stores!

Music in Our Lifetime (IV)- We're Surrounded!

Many artists, scientists, and environmentalists have written or talked about "noise" in the world (Appendix 7). In our American culture, one brand of "noise" is very prevalent: that is, of course, music!

If we go to the mall, we hear it in the main corridors and in each shop or department store: guaranteed to prompt us to buy. We play music in the car on long drives. Many students put their earphones on when they study or do assignments. We hear background music with the majority of ads on the TV.

We hear some music background in most films. We see more music in operas and musicals as a part of our community.

Isn't it obvious, in a course that appears complete, we must address "our" music of today?

It is good to look at several aspects,as DMX states in their sales material: music does have power in the total personality: mentally, emotionally, intellectually, it is not to be taken lightly. (Appendix 12, 13a,13b)

I generally looked at three aspects of our culture beyond listening for enjoyment-which is covered in the weekly "Listening session" (the reward time). Let's look at these possibilities:

A.   Advertisements/Business World-the power of music
B.   Musicals/Operas-Using words as well as music
C.   Movies/Dramas-Background-emotional setting

A. Advertisements

1.   Begin by bringing examples of ads for the class to hear.
     a.   Ask questions: What type of music is used?
     b.   What do you think is its purpose?
     c.   Could you do better?
2.   Collect a couple of CDs without singing or words on them-I used cuts from Santana's albums
3.   Divide the class into pairs: a speaker and someone to handle the background music.
4.   Have them make up an ad and write out the words. Then have them find music (no words) for the background. They are allowed to advertise for any fictional product (within reason!).
5.   They can then record when they're finished practicing. One of the most interesting ads was done by two eighth graders who tried to sell the "salmon slapper": he had a great line!
6.   You could have the students vote on the best ad, using two categories.
     a.   Best music background
     b.   Best story line

Again it's a recording session and class discipline is essential! REMEMBER, THE GOAL IS TO SHOW THE POWER OF THE MUSIC.

7. To again emphasize the goal, there are many articles of various web sites such as, "Playing with Aromas and Music, The New Marketing Weapon for Seducing Customers". (DMX at www.dmx.com/services, Appendix 13a,b)

They have found, "70% of retailers believe music increases sales"Look at their services:

    a. Rock Star Marketing
    b. DMX on site
    c. Music
    d. Video
    e. Scent
    f. Message
    g. Media Systems
    h. Customer Support
    i. Creation of an "emotional level" (DMX at www.dmx.com/services, Appendix 13ab)

Perhaps finish by having cd or video of some of the outstanding ads in the music classes and in society.

B. Musicals

I chose three musicals to work with: I could deal within my time frame and do that much. You may not have that much time so my suggestion is to pick the musical with the first being probably the best; etc. Music and words now combine to be a part of the communication (more emotion!). You may choose as you wish, but let me suggest some scenes of West Side Story.

    a. Jet Song (start with the beginning-great intro to ghetto)
    b. I want to be in America
    c. Gee, Officer Krupke

    d.   Dance at the gym

    e.   The rumble under the highway

    f.   Be Cool

    g.   Tony's Death

This is one of the most powerful musicals ever written. You need the original DVD (movie) version to get the full effect. When I was at my last middle school job, I presented this at least 48 times. No one ever complained! It does help to share what Bernstein was trying to say (or predict such as drugs, gang war, racism; etc).

Number Two, for me, would be Grease.

    a.   Start with the intro, and the Meeting at the Beach

    b.   Choose scenes which are relevant to the story, it needs to be previewed-you need to stay away from the school dance, the girls' slumber party; etc.

    c.   I didn't deal with the end of the story but pointed out several things such as importance of dance

Number Three, I did the Wiz!

The students really loved this one because of the appearance of Michael Jackson as the scarecrow-he does a great job! The portion of the movie-going to Oz and Dorothy's meeting her new friends and entering into the castle: great section, great acting. The yellow brick road with Scarecrow and Dorothy was great. Other than the color scenes in Oz, one could show more if students are interested. The writer really stresses family and friendship.

I stressed with the students the singing being the inner emotions and thoughts of the characters.

C. Movies/Drama (Background and Themes)

1. Choose a couple of movies that have background music which affects the emotional climate of the film.
   a. Discuss how the music affects the action
   b. Is there anything else in the movie that influences how o one feels?
2. Begin the project by sketching a simple "bad-good guy drama or melodrama. Perhaps 3-4 scenes at the most.
3. Have the students put music to the play. Try to have several old CDs they could use
4. Have groups of 5-7----actors, actresses, tech people.
   Have them video the play with music and do a playback. (Yes, someone needs a video camera).
5. Have the students record what they are doing and have discussion.

The project will take more time than the other assignments, my recommendation would be to do this one early on or wait until last and not worry about everyone finishing.

Music Activities

Music activities is a very limited chapter so to speak. The reason being, we don't have time to build motivation and get involved in complex instructions. You will generally find that even the youngest students will have some knowledge of music. You will generally find that even the youngest students will have a bit of basic knowledge of such things as tempo, timing, and a marvelous ear for rhythm and melody. Using that built-in ability, I had a tendency to limit music skills of a formal nature to things such as a rhythm contests-the winner receives some candy or other treat.

I had them learn to play "chop-sticks" on the piano and actually read the notes while doing it. I taught them how to read treble clef notes.

My students wanted to learn to play the first part of "Fur Elise" by Beethoven. We taught it.

That was all we did and all we had time for, with our other projects!

The main part of listening to formal music would be the early history work. There you play portions with explanation or description.

You may certainly add other fun things: using the "smart board" or computers for more technology projects if you wish. Develop. Make it more involved, more interactive, more hands on!

I taught one set of classes "swing dancing" when we were doing a 50's musical for our spring production!

Epilogue

The dictionary defines an epilogue as, "a short section at the end of a literary or dramatic work, often discussing the future of the characters".

So what is to be the future of our "characters", our students? Do they learn what music is all about, do they understand the power of music, the ability of music to serve as a creation medium, as a communication medium, as a healing medium! Is music just for a small group of elites performing to satisfy themselves? Is it not a left brain, right brain dilemma? We need balance in our lives: this makes music so important to our culture.

There are high schools in our state where music is out of the daily schedule: there might still be "music clubs"! There are vastly more middle schools where only band exists and perhaps a sort-of chorus or a performing class. Both music teachers and principals fear the typical try-it-formal music class where students are not interested and have no motivation! It is amazing what an activity centered, interactive class can do-discipline becomes less of a problem.

We are in a battle to preserve a highly important portion of our country's culture for the good of the population-our students-it will certainly be a challenge and will not come easy.

I wish you the best in this unique quest-go for it! You are welcome to communicate with me anytime-I'm glad to talk and help.

Lynn Howard
alyhow1@live.com

Bibliography

Colquhoun, Neil: Authors' Editor,
Volkerling, Michael: Publisher's Editor. Soundscape Series: Sound, Time, and Creatures. Wellington, N.Z.: Reed Education, 1975.

      Contributers:
      Jack Body
      Neil Colquhoun
      William Dart
      Colleen McCracken
      John Orams
      Laughton Pattrick
      Susan Rhind
      Michael Volkerling
Soundscape Series: Sound, Time, and Creatures

Daniels, Norman. Jansen, Guy E., Ed.. Sound and Sense: The Language of Music. Wellington, N.Z.: Reed Education, 1974.

Field, Dodgson, Robert. Jansen, Guy E., Ed.. Sound and Sense: The Literature of Music. Wellington, N.Z.: Reed Education, 1976.

Grunfield, Frederic V. and Editors of Time-Life Record. The Baroque Era. New York: Time Incorporated, 1965-8.

Heatley, Michael, General Editor. The Definitive Illustrated Encyclopedia of Rock. London: Flame Tree Publishing, 2006-2010.

Larsen, Maurice. Jansen, Guy E., Ed.. Sound and Sense: Aural Perception. Wellington, N.Z.: Reed Education, 1976.

Sell, David. Jansen, Guy E., Ed.. Sound and Sense: Musical Textures. Wellington, N.Z.: Reed Education, 1974.

Koster, Jan. Retrieved July, 2011 from http.//www.jsbach.org/biography. html htt

Retrieved July, 2011 from http://en.wikipedia.org/wiki/ Johann_Sebastian_Bach.

Retrieved Summer, 2011 from http://www. DMX About Us/Articles/ Why DMX Music/Services.

Retrieved, 2011, from the web site of the author's brother-in-law.

Retrieved Jan. 7, 2011 from two former students, GHS1972@yahoo groups.com.

Appendix

1a Graphic Composition

TIME	0 seconds→8	seconds→12	seconds→17	seconds→23	seconds→31	seconds→35	seconds→39	seconds→45
IDEA	"Love"	Interzone	"Anger"	Interzone	"Content-ment"	"Violence"	Interzone	"Peace"
SEC-TIONS	Middle Piano Black notes no chords	↓	Bottom Quarter White notes Chords	↓	Middle Piano	Middle and Lower Piano Black chords	↓	Upper Quarter Black notes White held chords
DY-NAM-ICS	Fairly soft	Increase volume	Loud	Decrease volume	Fairly soft	Very loud	Decrease volume	Soft
OTHER INSTRU-MENTS								

1b   Graphic Symbols

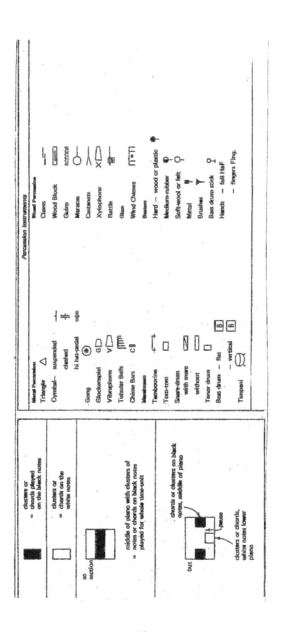

2a   New Zealand Graphic Composition

The Pheasant A poem by R.P. Tristram Coffin. Setting by Greg Caigou.

THE PHEASANT
Robert P. Tristram Coffin

A pheasant cock sprang into view,
A living jewel, up he flew.
His wings laid hold on empty space,
Scorn bulged his eyeballs out with grace.
He was a hymn from tail to beak,
With not a tender note or meek.
Then the gun let out its thunder,
The bird descended struck with wonder.
He ran a little, then amazed,
Settled with his head upraised,
The fierceness flowed out of his eyes
and left them meek and large and wise.
Gentleness relaxed his head,
He lay in jewelled feathers, dead.

Key to Symbols:

glissando   repeated notes
high register chords (clusters)   falling notes
low chords   shape of melody   paired notes
melody-in middle register. Position indicates register.

Tuned instruments:
Play only black notes
Empty unit = silence

2b New Zealand Graphic Composition, continued

NOVEMBER DAY
Eleanor Averitt

Old haggard wind has plucked the trees
Like pheasants, held between her knees.
In rows she hangs them, bare and neat,
Their brilliant plumage at her feet.

Conductor: The units have no time limit. Use an agreed signal to indicate change to next unit. Conductor indicates dynamics and instrumental balance to the players.
Note: Special lighting effects were used in a public performance of this composition.

3a Penderecki, Graphic Composition

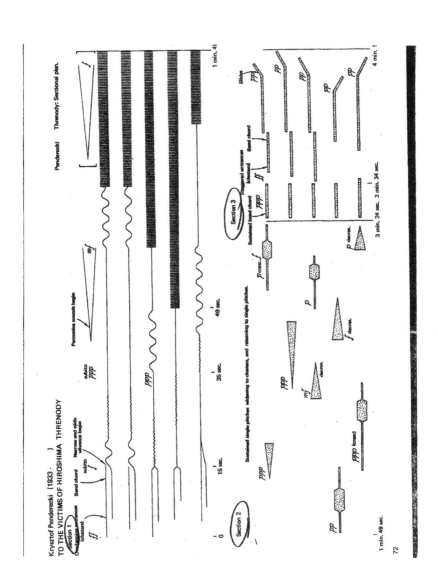

3b   Penderecki, continued

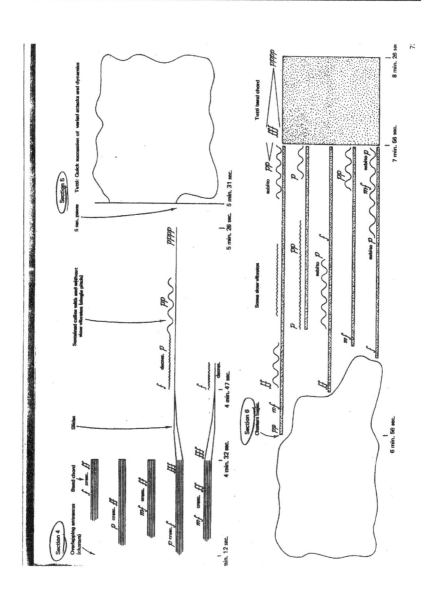

4 Photo of students during Graphic Composition

5   Example of Student-type of Graphic Composition

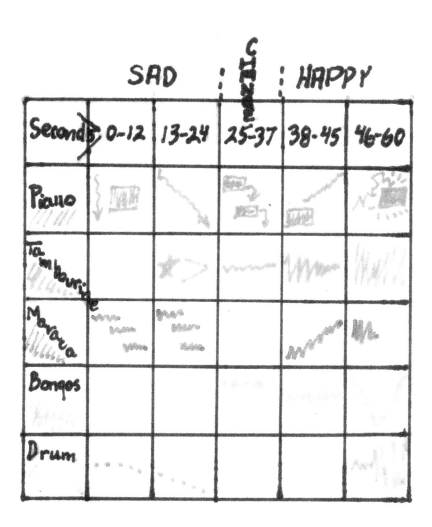

6 Possible creation for Graphic Composition

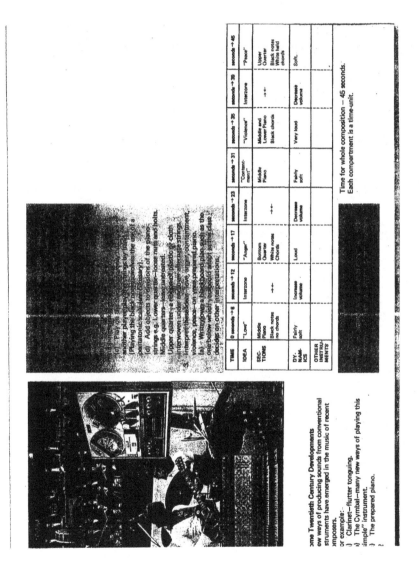

TIME	0 seconds → 6	seconds → 12	seconds → 17	seconds → 23	seconds → 31	seconds → 35	seconds → 39	seconds → 45
IDEA	"Low"	Interzone	"Anger"	Interzone	"Content-ment"	"Violence"	Interzone	"Peace"
SEC-TIONS	Middle Piano Black notes no chords	←→	Bottom Quarter White notes Chords	←→	Middle Piano	Middle and Lower Piano Black chords	←→	Upper Quarter Black notes White held chords
DY-NAM-ICS	Fairly soft	Increase volume	Loud	Decrease volume	Fairly soft	Very loud	Decrease volume	Soft
OTHER INSTRU-MENTS								

Time for whole composition — 45 seconds.
Each compartment is a time-unit.

...ome Twentieth Century Developments

...ew ways of producing sounds from conventional
...struments have emerged in the music of recent
...omposers.
...or example:
...) Clarinet—flutter tonguing.
...) The Cymbal—many new ways of playing this
...imple" instrument.
...) The prepared piano.

7 Noise Pollution by Dr. H.B. Turbott

NOISE POLLUTION

1. Noise Pollution Is Growing

It is belatedly being realised that noise is as much a threat to health as polluted air and water. In industry this is now accepted, following a good deal of education from the Department of Health, and the example set to industry by hearing conservation programmes in the sixties throughout the Public Service and associated industries such as the Railways. Audiometers were used for screening noise levels. Where this was excessive one or more or many things had to be done—machinery redesigned, silencers fitted, sound barriers erected to contain noise, soundproof observation booths constructed, or other noise reducing methods used, such as reducing shift times and rotating duties.

This preventive work revealed that noise had been neglected for too long, as one in five industrial work places had potential noise hazards and three in ten apprentices suffered hearing damage. A step forward was the Worker's Compensation Amendment Act1970, which introduced compensation for deafness due to noise at work. The result has been the establishment of hearing conservation programmes in industry. The National Audiology Centre in Auckland gives special training to industrial medical officers, doctors, nurses and safety personnel in screening for noise, selecting and fitting ear plugs and so on.

While industry is now awake to the damage of noise, the rest of the community is insufficiently aware. The Board of Health has set up a committee on noise which will gather facts about the noise risk in the community. Their findings will give a guideline about noise.

A guideline is needed. Local authority workers using pneumatic drills are subjected to the decibel level of a drill which is 120 or pain level; the farm worker does not seem to be alive to the possibility of hearing damage from noisy tractors. Chain saws are a common tool and those who use them often are likely to cause damage to their hearing unless protective measures are taken.

In cities the roar of traffic is a noise pollutant. You can become accustomed to it but his continuous roar nevertheless probably affects the acuity of hearing. For sound sleep your bedroom should not register more than 30 decibels, but even in towns and cities the noise goes higher than this at some time during the night, with peaks caused by party-going, cars and motor cycles that reach 90 and over.

Ninety decibels is enough noise for our ears. Motor cycles at 110 decibels, pop music at the average level of 114 and often reaching 120, are examples of community noise pollution.

Noise also affects the nervous system. A background of loud noises reduces the ability to concentrate and in factories it has been demonstrated that when the noise level is lowered productivity is increased, mistakes are less frequent, accidents are fewer and absenteeism is reduced. Noise can be a cause of headaches and helps to build up nervous tension. A high decibel level of noise over a period of time will make the heart beat faster and raise blood pressure. For the sake of our hearing and general health we must recognise noise and take steps against it as a dangerous pollutant.

Dr H.B. Turbott, *New Zealand Listener*

8a   Typical history outline:
Johann Sebastian Bach/Baroque Period

My notes on preparing the outline for the students. A formal outline
would have to be built. Use selections from Brandenburg Concerto and
Magnificat in D Major. Check Bach's life in the Wikipedia..excellent.
Show Baroque pictures(Appendix 8b).

Baroque Johann Sebastian Bach / G.F. George Frederick Handel
Period -
1685-1750   1. instrumental music - own right
             2. figured Bass — basso continuo
             3. Solo instruments   {length} {opera
             4. Larger compositions {texture}   {mass
             5. Contrast {Melody - free
                        {Bass - structured
    Bart!!   6. Reflects the period - More ornate
Dalhci zete.- 7. Accent on form
             8. New (wood) instruments - unique!
             9. Driving aggressive pace, strong beats
12. Development
of organ chord 10. Still predominance of music in
harpsi   the church venue (past history)
                    a. nobility - educated -
                       madrigals
by word   b. peasantry - traditional
n singing   - passed on - folk songs
           11. Music begins to break out of Church
               venue

55

8b Typical history outline:
Johann Sebastian Bach/Baroque Period, continued

SIGNPOST ON AN AUSTRIAN INN

The
Baroque
Look

ENGLISH CLOCK

10

In all the arts the baroque style had the force of an explosion. In place of Renaissance restraint, repose and symmetry, baroque introduced intensity, tension and, above all, movement. In baroque fountains, for example, architects molded moving water as though it were clay, setting thin jets and arcs against massive cascades. In its last phases, the baroque gradually evolved into the style we know as "rococo"; the majesty of baroque at its high point evolved into ornate charm. Baroque and rococo artists and craftsmen all shared a common goal: to achieve exuberant splendor in decoration. Thus there is a strong continuity of approach and achievement in baroque and rococo, evident in the clocks and other objects shown here no less than in the churches pictured on the following pages. Though they span almost two centuries of design and construction, these churches are alike in enshrining the deity in a setting of theatrical splendor.

GERMAN CUP

8c Typical history outline: Johann Sebastian Bach/Baroque Period, continued

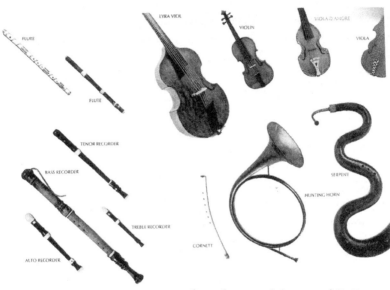

LYRA VIOL

VIOLIN

VIOLA D'AMORE

VIOLA

FLUTE

FLUTE

TENOR RECORDER

BASS RECORDER

SERPENT

HUNTING HORN

TREBLE RECORDER

CORNETT

ALTO RECORDER

An Assemblage of Music

Though no single work would call for all the instruments shown here, each, with its own tonal specialty, was available to the baroque composer. Some came from earlier eras and died during the baroque; others were created then and have survived in modified forms.

THE FLUTES. The group of recorders shown at the lower left above, derived from medieval piping instruments, produced the most common flute sounds of the baroque era. These are vertical, or "end-blown" flutes—that is, the player blows along the length of the flute's tube. Toward the end of the baroque period, the soft-voiced vertical flutes gave way to the louder and more penetrating "transverse" flutes *(upper left)*, which evolved from a shrill 16th century military instrument used in marching bands. The player of the transverse flute blows across a hole near the end of the instrument, holding the tube at right angles to his mouth; modern developments of this flute are equipped with a complex system of keys which enable a performer to play his instrument with greater precision and agility.

THE BOWED STRINGS. The baroque era brought the violin (at top, above) to a peak of perfection; no subsequent craftsman has ever surpassed the work of Cremonese masters like Amati, Guarnieri and Stradivari. But other bowed instruments of the baroque have not survived. Throughout the period, for example, composers wrote for light-bodied instruments descended from the "viols" and known as violas da gamba (literally, "of the leg"). These were not modern violas of the violin family (an example of a true viola is shown next to the viola da gamba above); the violas da gamba were merely "viols" held between the legs. They were eventually superseded by the louder and fuller-toned members of the violin family. Other bowed instruments now obsolete were the lyra viol, which had a fingerboard like a modern guitar's, and—strangest of all, perhaps—the viola d'amore, which had both the usual bowed strings and an additional set of *unbowed* strings, stretched under the fingerboard. In much the way that a window pane will rattle when a truck or airplane passes by, these unbowed strings vibrated "sympathetically" with the bowed ones, enveloping every tone with a low buzz of sound.

THE PLUCKED STRINGS. The viola d'amore's principle of sympathetic vibration was applied to some extent in plucked instruments *(top, right)* like the theorbo and the huge chitarrone, in which additional strings ran under or

24

57

9a Profiles of Baroque, Classical, Romantic/20th Century Periods
Taken from Sound and Sense

PROFILE OF BAROQUE STYLE

- Alive and energetic.
- More ornate than earlier period.
- High degree of contrasts (high low, loud soft, large, small).
- Unflagging tempos.
- Continuous ever-present bass movement.
- Forceful metrical rhythms.
- Strong sense of key centre (major/minor)
- Melody activated by simple rhythms.
- Melody short and plain or long and spun out.
- Polyphonic texture predominates.

- Large spacious forms *viz* Vocal—*opera, oratorio, cantata, mass;* Instrumental—*concerto, sonata, overture, suite, fugue.*
- Stringed instruments predominate.
- Also harpsichord, flute, recorder, organ.
- Instrumental timbre gained importance.
- Improvisation reached peak of refinement.
- Instruments used for musical imagery
- Predominance of figured bass.

BAROQUE PERIOD

TITLE	COMPOSER	FORM	SOURCE (AUTHOR)
1. MESSIAH And the Glory of the Lord	Handel	Oratorio	Min. Score
2. SUITE NO. 2 IN B MINOR Second Movement	Bach	Suite Rondo	Noel Long
3. SUITE NO. 3 IN D Air	Bach	Suite	Roger Fiske Book I
4. BRANDENBURG CONCERTO NO. 2 Second Movement	Bach	Concerto Grosso	Roger Fiske
5. FIREWORKS MUSIC Two Minuets	Handel	Ternary	Noel Long
6. VIOLIN CONCERTO IN A MINOR First Movement	Bach	Concerto	Noel Long Book III
7. CHRISTMAS CONCERTO IN G MINOR	Corelli	Concerto Grosso	Roger Fiske Book III
8. OBOE CONCERTO IN B FLAT NO. 1 First Movement	Handel	Concerto	Roger Fiske Book III
9. TRUMPET CONCERTO Second Movement	Handel	Concerto	Roger Fiske Book I
10. MASS IN B MINOR Et In Carnatus Est (Credo)	Bach	Mass	Nadeau & Tesson

9b Profiles of Baroque, Classical, Romantic/20th Century Periods
Taken from Sound and Sense, continued

PROFILE OF CLASSICAL STYLES

- ☐ Thinning down of sound.
- ☐ Atmosphere less important.
- ☐ Highly refined and polished.
- ☐ Ideals of balance, symmetry and clarity.
- ☐ Gradual use of rise and fall in dynamics. (*cresc.* and *dim.*)
- ☐ Concert orchestra developed.
- ☐ Absence of *basso-continuo.*
- ☐ Melodies singable and easily recalled.
- ☐ Single melodies given importance.
- ☐ Melodies defined to fit four-bar phrase.

- ☐ Punctuated by cadences.
- ☐ Strong key relationships.
- ☐ Shift from elaborate polyphony to small homophonic texture.
- ☐ Clear transparent vertical textures.
- ☐ Clear-cut forms evolved.
- ☐ Favoured forms *sonata, rondo, ternary, minuet and trio, theme and variations.*
- ☐ Preference for symphony, chamber music, sonatas, opera.

CLASSICAL PERIOD

	TITLE	COMPOSER	FORM	SOURCE (AUTHOR)
1.	QUARTET OP 76 NO 3 (EMPEROR) Second Movement	Haydn	Quartet Air & Variations	Noel Long
2.	MARRIAGE OF FIGARO Aria: *Non Piu Andrai*	Mozart	Opera Aria	Min. Score
3.	PIANO CONCERTO NO 3 C MINOR First Movement	Beethoven	Concerto Sonata Form	Roger Fiske Book III
4.	OBOE QUARTET Third Movement	Mozart	Quartet Rondo	Noel Long
5.	PIANO CONCERTO NO 1 C Third Movement	Beethoven	Concerto Rondo	Noel Long
6.	SYMPHONY NO 39 IN E FLAT Third Movement	Mozart	Symphony Minuet & Trio	Roger Fiske Book II
7.	CLARINET QUINTET K581 FINALE Third Movement	Mozart	Quintet Theme & variations Minuet & Trio	Roger Fiske Book II
8.	*MAGIC FLUTE* OVERTURE Overture	Mozart	Overture to Opera	Noel Long
9.	SYMPHONY NO 104 *(LONDON)* Finale	Haydn	Symphony Sonata Form	Nadeau & Tesson
10.	SYMPHONY NO 7 First Movement	Beethoven	Symphony Sonata Form	Nadeau & Tesson

9c Profiles of Baroque, Classical, Romantic/20th Century Periods
Taken from Sound and Sense, continued

PROFILE OF ROMANTIC STYLES

- ☐ More personal and emotional.
- ☐ Sense of dramatic developed.
- ☐ Composer explores physical world and other arts.
- ☐ Longer dynamic curves to climaxes.
- ☐ Greater breadth and weight of sound.
- ☐ Deep sonorous timbres.
- ☐ Orchestra grows to massive size.
- ☐ Instrumental viruosity increases.
- ☐ Piano becomes favoured instrument.
- ☐ Rhythms stronger and freer.

- ☐ Spectacular climaxes.
- ☐ Melody more lyrical and expansive.
- ☐ Melody and harmony very chromatic.
- ☐ Richer more dissonant harmony.
- ☐ Prominent use of minor key.
- ☐ Striking harmonic effects.
- ☐ Texture thick and rich. '
- ☐ Predominant homophonic texture.
- ☐ Emphasis on miniature forms.

ROMANTIC PERIOD

TITLE	COMPOSER	FORM	SOURCE (AUTHOR)
1. ACADEMIC FESTIVAL OVERTURE	Brahms	Overture Concert	Min. Score
2. UNFINISHED SYMPHONY NO 8 First Movement	Schubert	Symphony Sonata Form	Roger Fiske
3. HEBRIDES OVERTURE	Mendelssohn	Overture Concert	Noel Long
4. THE ERL-KING	Schubert	Lied	Min. Score
5. MASTERSINGERS OVERTURE	Wagner	Overture Operatic	Noel Long
6. SERENADE IN D OP 11 Minuet–Scherzo	Brahms	Scherzo & Trio	Roger Fiske Book II
7. PIANO CONCERTO A MINOR First Movement	Grieg	Concerto	Roger Fiske Book III
8. SYMPHONY FANTASTIQUE Fifth Movement	Berlioz	Programme Symphony	Nadeau & Tesson
9. SIEGFRIED IDYLL	Wagner	Expanded Ternary	Nadeau & Tesson
10. DEATH & THE MAIDEN QUARTET Second Movement	Schubert	String Quartet Lied	Nadeau & Tesson

Surprise Symphony –

9d Profiles of Baroque, Classical, Romantic/20th Century Periods Taken from Sound and Sense, continued

PROFILE OF TWENTIETH CENTURY STYLES

- ☐ New treatment of basic elements.
- ☐ High degree of tension.
- ☐ Marked use of unusual combinations.
- ☐ Voice and instrument explored in ensemble.
- ☐ Prominent use of wind instruments.
- ☐ Traditional tone qualities distorted.
- ☐ New twelve-tone technique recognised.
- ☐ Rhythm increasingly irregular, non-metrical and complex.
- ☐ Polyrhythms exploited.
- ☐ Disjunct melody line, wide leaps.
- ☐ Melody dominated by instrumental idiom.
- ☐ Melody often short and fragmented.
- ☐ Dissonance exploited.
- ☐ Use of bitonal, polytonal and atonal qualities and non-traditional scale patterns.
- ☐ Contrapuntal texture exploited.
- ☐ Continued use of longer forms.

TWENTIETH CENTURY

	TITLE	COMPOSER	FORM	SOURCE (AUTHOR)
1.	*FIREBIRD* SUITE Finale	Stravinsky	Ballet Suite	Min. Score
2.	SERENADE FOR TENOR, HORN, STRINGS *The Splendour Falls*	Britten	Song	Min. Score
3.	*THRENODY TO THE VICTIMS OF HIROSHIMA* (Graphic Composition Appendix(e))	Penderecki	Tone Poem	Min. Score
4.	PSALM 150	Britten	Ternary Form	Full Score
5.	SYMPHONY NO 1 First Movement	Shostakovich	Symphony	Noel Long
6.	*EL SALON MEXICO*	Copland	Free Sonata Form	Noel Long
7.	*RITE OF SPRING* Intro: Dance of Youth & Maidens	Stravinsky	Ballet Suite	Serposs & Singleton
8.	*LA MER* First Movement	Debussy	Symphonic Sketches	Nadeau & Tesson
9.	L' HISTOIRE DU SOLDAT Three Dances	Stravinsky	Dance Forms	Nadeau & Tesson
10.	VIOLIN CONCERTO First Movement	Berg	Concerto	Nadeau & Tesson

10a An interesting story about music in our culture

THE SITUATION

In Washington , DC , at a Metro Station, on a cold January morning in 2007, this man with a violin played six Bach pieces for about 45 minutes. During that time, approximately 2,000 people went through the station, most of them on their way to work. After about 3 minutes, a middle-aged man noticed that there was a musician playing. He slowed his pace and stopped for a few seconds, and then he hurried on to meet his schedule.

About 4 minutes later:

The violinist received his first dollar. A woman threw money in the hat and, without stopping, continued to walk.

At 6 minutes:

A young man leaned against the wall to listen to him, then looked at his watch and started to walk again.

At 10 minutes:

A 3-year old boy stopped, but his mother tugged him along hurriedly. The kid stopped to look at the violinist again, but the mother pushed hard and the child continued to walk, turning his head the whole time. This action was repeated by several other children, but every parent - without exception - forced their children to move on quickly.

10b An interesting story about music in our culture, continued

At 45 minutes:

The musician played continuously. Only 6 people stopped and listened for a short while. About 20 gave money but continued to walk at their normal pace. The man collected a total of $32.

After 1 hour:

He finished playing and silence took over. No one noticed and no one applauded. There was no recognition at all.

No one knew this, but the violinist was **Joshua Bell**, one of the greatest musicians in the world. He played one of the most intricate pieces ever written, with a violin worth $3.5 million dollars. Two days before, Joshua Bell sold-out a theater in Boston where the seats averaged $100 each to sit and listen to him play the same music.

This is a true story. Joshua Bell, playing incognito in the D.C. Metro Station, was organized by the Washington Post as part of a social experiment about **perception, taste and people's priorities.**

This experiment raised several questions:

*In a common-place environment, at an inappropriate hour, do we perceive beauty?

*If so, do we stop to appreciate it?

*Do we recognize talent in an unexpected context?

One possible conclusion reached from this experiment could be this:

If we do <u>not</u> have a moment to stop and listen to one of the best musicians in the world, playing some of the finest music ever written, with one of the most beautiful instruments ever made . . ..

How many other things are we missing as we rush through life?

Enjoy life NOW .. it has an expiration date

11 Written by one of my former students, graduated in (1972)

From: Debbie McGavran (debbiem@landscapemgmt.com)
To: GHS1972@yahoogroups.com;
Date: Fri, January 7, 2011 7:50:02 AM
Cc:
Subject: RE: [GHS1972] Perception

John one thing I hold close to my heart is music. Anytime someone is playing anywhere my senses take over and I stop and listen. The world is to tied up with their ipods, computers, iphones etc. Music can reach deep into your soul and express every feeling that you may have ever felt. This is not exclusive to music it could be a beautiful day, a friend, a river or lake, the mountains. Just stop and look what God gave us and give thanks for the opportunity to enjoy.

☺

From: GHS1972@yahoogroups.com [mailto:GHS1972@yahoogroups.com] **On Behalf Of johnny flambay**
Sent: Tuesday, January 04, 2011 6:29 PM
Subject: [GHS1972] Perception

Perception. I absolutely love this.

12   DMX Introduction

DMX

About Us

Articles

DMX provides sensory branding elements of sights, sounds and scents unique to your business. Forward-thinking businesses are now embracing integrated multi-sensory elements designed by DMX experts that catch the attention of the media again and again.

DMX - Why DMX Music

Be experienced

Let customers actually experience your brand with highly customized in-store sonic solutions that capture the personality of your brand or business.

Control your environment

Ensure your customer experience is consistent from visit to visit and your music meets your goals.

Influence behavior

Clear tables faster. Get customers to linger longer. Make time fly. Excite, sooth or move. It's not magic. It's the power of music.

Keep it legal

Relax. DMX handles all required music licensing through thousands of relationships with critical industry players, including labels, performing rights organizations (ASCAP, BMI and SoundExchange) and publishers.

13a DMX Brings customers to Their Senses

DMX

Services

DMX Brings Customers to Their Senses

DMX is an industry pioneer with over 35 years of experience providing on-site marketing solutions to businesses of all types and sizes. Every DMX solution is completely customized according to the specific needs of each business. And DMX is a single-source provider, offering music, video, scent and messaging solutions, along with new Web and mobile applications to help businesses expand their reach.

The result? Our clients get completely immersive experiences that genuinely reflect their brands. They get integrated experiences, consistent and authentic everywhere they turn up. DMX solutions connect with customers, build loyalty and help businesses succeed. Discover what DMX can do for you.

MUSIC

Expertly designed music experiences set the mood and engage customers on an emotional level. On-site, online and on-the-go solutions to meet all of your needs.
Learn More ›

13b DMX Brings customers to Their Senses, continued

VIDEO

HD imagery and music videos captivate, entertain and deliver that indispensable cool factor.
Learn More ›

SCENT

Cutting-edge scent experiences help distinguish brands and foster powerful emotional
bonds.
Learn More ›

MESSAGE

Innovative messaging solutions help businesses stay in touch with customers on-site, on the
phone and on the go.
Learn More ›

MEDIA SYSTEMS

State-of-the-art multimedia systems for any environment – from retail stores to resorts and
casinos – deliver captivating sensory experiences.
Learn More ›

14a Sample Schedules for General Music

Sample Schedules for General Music

EARLY IN QUARTER/SEMESTER, OR.......

MONDAY-Focus on Can You Listen? Discuss goals for the week(or what ever period of time)- try to find music to signal passing from one activity to another

TUESDAY-Introduce instruments available and in the area, piano, discuss respect; etc. Show sound system, review the listening material

WEDNESDAY- Intro. Examples of graphic composition, discuss the how and why, Set up groups(4-5) Talk about organization within the group, Care of materials

THURSDAY- History of Music(outline to copy and music to playj)

FRIDAY- Listening day-students bring-no cussing- "DJ" runs the choices

FURTHER ON.....

MONDAY-further on the listening material, test on some sounds, look at photos-what sounds would be there?

TUESDAY-Review the goal in Graphic Comp. Goals for the week, review listening skills —Last day to prepare for recording session

WEDNESDAY- Recording Session(Graphic Comp.), Discuss each comp. as committee finishes(Did they succeed in achieving goals?)

THURSDAY- History of Music-build portfolio with the outlines and notes and activities

FRIDAY- Listening Day

14b Sample Schedules for General Music, continued

NEAR END..

MONDAY-Listening, Sound test, Goals

TUESDAY- Share material on DMX, Start preparing own "advertisements" to record, partner work(Choose background music-no words, work out a phony product)

WEDNESDAY- Record the ads that are ready/further work-give others a chance to rerecord next week

THURSDAY- History of Music(outline, portfolio), music examples(short!)

FRIDAY- Listening Day

Appendix Footnotes

1a and 1b
Norman Daniels, Sound and Sense: The Language of Music, 12-13.

2a and 2b
Norman Daniels, Sound and Sense: The Language of Music, 26, 17.

3a and 3b
Maurice Larson, Sound and Sense: Aural Perception, 72, 73.

6
David Sell, Sound and Sense: Musical Textures, 45.

7
Norman Daniels, Sound and Sense: Aural Perception, 58.

8a
Author

8b
Frederic V. Grunfield, Ed., The Baroque Era, 10, 23, 24.

9a, 9b, 9c, and 9d
Maurice Larsen, Sound and Sense: Aural Perception, 64, 66, 68, and 70.

10a, 10b

Story sent to author by his brother-in-law, January, 2011.

11

Comments by two former students of the author.

12, 13a, 13b

DMX About Us; etc.

14

Sample Schedules for General Music

Made in the USA
Monee, IL
28 December 2020